Pam, Sam and Tam

By Cameron Macintosh

Sam sits at the mat.

Tam sits at the mat.

Pam is at the mat.

Pam tips.

Sam sips!

Tam taps.

It tips!

Sam and Tam sit.

Pam pats Sam and Tam.

Sip, sip, sip!

CHECKING FOR MEANING

1. Who pours the water? *(Literal)*

2. Who tips over the water? *(Literal)*

3. How do you think Tam is feeling when Sam is sipping the water? *(Inferential)*

EXTENDING VOCABULARY

sits	What is the base of the word *sits*? Why is there an *s* added to the base? Why doesn't the base have an *s* on it in *Sam and Tam sit*?
tips	Look at the word *tips*. Find another word in the story that rhymes with *tips*. What other words can you think of that rhyme with these words?
taps	Look at the word *taps*. What does the word *taps* mean in this story? What else can it mean?

MOVING BEYOND THE TEXT

1. Why does Pam give Sam and Tam water to drink? What do people drink that cats should not drink?

2. What is your favourite thing to drink?

3. What else do you think Pam does to take care of Sam and Tam?

4. What are some other things you can do with water?

SPEED SOUNDS

Mm	Ss	Aa	Pp	Ii	Tt

PRACTICE WORDS

Sam

sits

at

Pam

mat

It

sips

Tam

sit

tips

taps

pats

sip

Sip